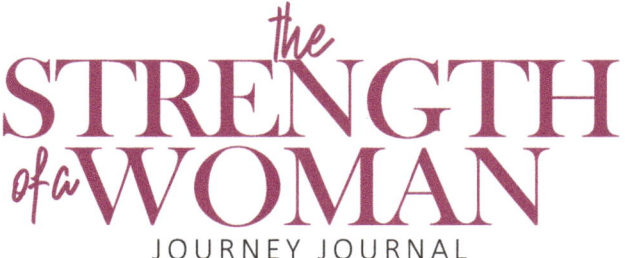

the STRENGTH of a WOMAN
JOURNEY JOURNAL

BY KIMBERLY R. LOCK

A WOMAN 2 WOMAN
PRESENTATION

THE STRENGTH OF A WOMAN: JOURNEY JOURNAL
Copyright © 2018 Kimberly R. Lock

All rights reserved. No part of this book may be reproduced or transmitted in any form or by any means, electronic or mechanical, including photocopying, recording, or by any information storage and retrieval system without the written permission of the author or publisher, except where permitted by law.

ISBN: 978-1-949176-24-7 (paperback)

Edited by: Tecia Sellers
Exterior Cover Design by: Money Graphics LLC
Interior Design by: Anita Clinton Enterprises LLC
Published by: KRL Publishing

Introduction

Hello, Woman. If you are reading this, you have made the decision to clear your mind of any preconceived notions, to open your heart to transparency, and to strengthen your core. This journey is about you, woman. What you desire to receive is what you will obtain. As with anything, the results are based upon the effort.

This "journey" journal is about supporting your efforts to discover who you are in the Lord and living out your purpose to the fullest intent. Some of us have derailed and sabotaged our attempts at living a purpose-driven life by listening to the voices connected to us, or the voices within our own heads. By the end of your journey journal, it is my sincerest prayer that the only voice you are allowing to direct your path is that of the Holy Spirit.

Have you ever heard the statement: "It is not about the destination, it is about the journey?" While this may be true, I believe that if the journey is filled with unclear directions, improper attire, and incomplete instructions on where you are going, you will never reach the intended destination. Your destiny. I believe that it is impossible to know where you are going and who is going with you, if you do not know who you are.

DEAR WOMAN:

Your prognosis has been given and it does not look good. Although it was not what you anticipated, the MRI suggests

that open heart surgery is necessary, as there may be some reparation that is required to fix the damage done to your heart. This operation requires the surgeon, Jesus, to open your chest and access your heart. The Holy Spirit is putting on His scrubs, surgical gloves and hair net. He has prepared the surgical room with all the necessary equipment. Don't worry, you are in good hands. My assignment is to ensure that you follow the steps outlined in this journal, as your procedural guide, to ensure the results of the surgery are successful. You will be given a goal, scripture, and affirmation to support your surgical procedure. An affirmation is a positive declaration made by you, to encourage you. If you have not created any before, I encourage you to jot down all the affirmations given in this journal. Repeat them and allow them to become a part of who you are.

We will use the anatomy of an apple to get to the core of who you are. Are you ready? Let's begin!

PART ONE
the Skin

— the Skin —

GOAL:
LOVE THE SKIN THAT YOU ARE IN

THE Skin OF THE APPLE

It comes in various colors: green, yellow, red, various shades of red, and even a multi-color of red and yellow. The color of an apple often determines the sweetness of the apple. For example, we know that Granny-Smith apples are green and most likely will have a more tartness to their flavoring than a Honey-Crisp apple, which is a combo of red/yellow.

The skin of an apple serves a few key purposes:

1. Protect and prolong the life of the apple.
2. Protect the pulp (the white part that we eat) of the apple.
3. Provide additional nutrients – if I eat the skin, I'm receiving a sample of the full nutrients that the pulp of the apple provides. So basically, what is inside of the apple, has to show up on the outside. (Come on in the room people!)
4. The skin of the apple also can absorb toxins from pesticides.

THE *Skin* OF THE HUMAN

Like the apple skin, our skin serves similar purposes:

1. Protect our bodies against external irritations.
2. Regulate our body temperatures.
3. Prevent the loss of blood and body fluids.

WOMAN 2 WOMAN

Listennnn!!!! This skin stuff gets a lot of us in trouble. Whether we recognize it or not, a lot of what we do centers around skin color.

Go with me here for a minute.

Remember when you were in middle school, your friends thought that one dude was "fine." You know, the popular one? His looks were "alright" to you. You didn't think he was all that cute. By the time you got to high school, you had a vivid depiction of what "fine" meant to you:

"Girl, he gone be tall (we didn't know about inches – it was either tall, medium, or short), natural curly hair, light-brown yes and... (here it comes)

Brown-skinned
Or
Light-skinned"

And the correct pronunciation of "skinned" is skindid – thank you very much!

YES. YOU. DID! You KNOW you did that. Well, I did. Subliminally, as you journeyed through life, you sought for a man who fit that description. The seed had been planted and you planted

that seed of your ideal man. That young man could have all the other features/traits but if the skin tone was not to your liking, you shriveled up your nose and questioned if he was the "one" because you had a list.

There is a saying: "Beauty is only skin deep." This implies that the physical features of an individual are not as important as the intellectual, emotional, and spiritual qualities; however, I would like to add that just as the skin of the apple contains a subset of the nutrients found within the apple, your outward appearance should also reflect who you are inwardly. Someone should be able to look at you and say: "There is something different about you." Yes sirrrr, it is the anointing and it is attractive. When you are anointed, people can tell the difference. They may be unable to explain it, and you probably cannot either, but they can see it. It's all on your skin. It's written all over your face. Listen here! When Moses came from receiving the 10 commandments from God and being in His presence, his face was shining with the glory of God (Exodus 34:29). After being in the presence of God, because the others were afraid to come near him, Moses had to place a veil over his face...huhhhhh??? Come ONN Sirrr!!! Now that is what I call a "son-bathing."

The intent of the human skin is to protect the body, fight against external irritation, prevent the loss of blood and body fluids. WOMAN – let's begin to use our skin for its intended purpose.

Girl, you gone have to put on some "Son" block. Where we trying to go, we do not have time to back track and live in cycles of depression, loneliness, and hurt. What is "Son"

block? Jesus. Put on Jesus.

Romans 13:14 (NKJV)
But put on the Lord Jesus Christ, and make no provision for the flesh, to fulfill its lusts.

I shared with you the functions and purpose of the skin. This is what you need to do:

1. Protect Your Body From External Irritations.

    SIN IS "irra." The young folks' terminology for irritating. Cover up your skin. When your skin is exposed too much, you'll experience some burning. Cover it up; it sends a message to that man and sends the wrong chemical to your brain. You feel sexy and he feels lucky. Why? Because of that blouse. That blouse is cute, but if the crease of your boobies is showing — you know, the line that separates the one boobie from the other... (they need to make a way for authors to use emojis because I would use the "eyes-wide open" and looking off to the left emoji right now) get a camisole.

    If that line that separates the one cheek from the other is exposed when you bend over, and your pretty little purple laced-top undies can be seen, you gotta get a cute belt to keep those pants in the right place, at the right time (emoji eyes).

2. Regulate Your Temperature

    You know you have no business going around that man. You and your mind had an entire conversation about what happened before. If what took place

before did not involve the word of God, deliverance from sin, and praying in the name of Jesus – do not go. Why are you accessible after business hours to be called or text? And do not go on his Instagram page either. You prayed that nighttime prayer not even thinking about Jesus. Use your "Son" block.

3. Prevent the loss of blood and body fluid
   (multiple instances of emoji eyes inserted here)
   Soul ties are real, woman. To be chosen, you must choose yourself first.

   I Corinthians 3:16 says that we are the temple of God. Why didn't the scripture say we are the home of God? Why didn't the scripture say that we are the house of God? Why didn't the scripture say that we are the shelter, the chamber, lodge or camp of God?

   A house is where a family resides. It is only the structure for shelter. A temple is a sanctuary- a house of worship, a place devoted to a special purpose; a place regarded as holy.

   Your body is the temple of God; He regarded our bodies as being holy, devoted and designed for a special purpose! A temple is like a shrine – it is a sacred place and that is what your body is – it is sacred, and it is THE ONLY place on this Earth where God's Holy Spirit lives, and it is also where you worship, honor and reverence our Savior, Jesus. That is why it is CRITICAL that we value ourselves – our temple as a place of honor.

SCRIPTURE:

Psalm 139:13-16 The Message (MSG)
Oh yes, you shaped me first inside, then out; you formed me in my mother's womb. I thank you, High God—you're breathtaking! Body and soul, I am marvelously made! I worship in adoration—what a creation! You know me inside and out, you know every bone in my body;

You know exactly how I was made, bit by bit, how I was sculpted from nothing into something.

Like an open book, you watched me grow from conception to birth; all the stages of my life were spread out before you, the days of my life all prepared before I'd even lived one day.

AFFIRMATION

- I choose me because God chose me.
- He created me. He designed me.
- He purposed me.
- I embrace every imperfection that I perceive in the appearance of my skin.
- I am purposed to fulfill the purpose my Father intently created through my existence, and my skin has NOTHING to do with it.
- I. LOVE. ME.

SELF-EXAMINATION

Thinking must be intentional. Really think about these questions as you examine yourself.

1. Who are you?
2. What are willing to leave behind to be who you are supposed to be?
3. What will it take to be the best you?

Note: What's inside of you, will show up on the outside.

Reflections

Reflections

_____
_____
_____
_____
_____
_____
_____
_____
_____
_____
_____
_____
_____
_____
_____
_____
_____
_____

Reflections

Reflections

_____

_____

_____

_____

_____

_____

_____

_____

_____

_____

_____

_____

_____

_____

_____

_____

_____

_____

_____

Reflections

_____
_____
_____
_____
_____
_____
_____
_____
_____
_____
_____
_____
_____
_____
_____
_____
_____
_____

Reflections

_____
_____
_____
_____
_____
_____
_____
_____
_____
_____
_____
_____
_____
_____
_____
_____
_____
_____
_____
_____

Reflections

PART TWO
the Stem

— the Stem —

GOAL: REMAIN CONNECTED

THE *Stem* OF THE APPLE

The stem of an apple contains nutrients such as fiber and iron. Not only does it hold the core of the apple together, but also, the stem anchors the apple onto the tree as it continues to grow. When an apple is ripe and ready to be eaten, it falls from the tree, along with the stem.

THE *Stem* OF THE HUMAN

The stem connects the apple to the tree. This reminds me of the umbilical cord within the womb of a mother who is with child. The umbilical cord connects the child to the mother. The child receives nutrients and blood to survive, while in this womb, through this connection. Spiritually speaking, our stem connector is the Holy Spirit. Jesus is the vine (the life, the sustainer, the roots that run through the tree) and God Himself is the tree. When the apple has fallen from the tree, it bears remnants of its connection to the tree by the stem.

In other words, we have been physically separated from our home. Our citizenship is the Kingdom of Heaven. There should be some remnant or connection to our home. There

should be some sign that we are in this world, but not of this world — that sign is through the Holy Spirit. The Bible says if we do not have the Spirit of Christ, we are not His:

Romans 8:9 Amplified Bible (AMP)
However, you are not [living] in the flesh [controlled by the sinful nature] but in the Spirit, if in fact the Spirit of God lives in you [directing and guiding you]. But if anyone does not have the Spirit of Christ, he does not belong to Him [and is not a child of God].

WOMAN 2 WOMAN

Your citizenship is that of a kingdom, where you are royalty. When you think of royalty, what comes to mind? Imagine one of power, wealthy, a rich heritage and lineage of historical figures whose works and causes shaped the future. There is a quiet confidence in knowing that whatever comes up against you, it will be handled. There is a badge of honor and respect to protect the legacy, the lineage and the Kingdom at all cost. There are just some behaviors and actions that would be totally out of character as representatives of the Kingdom, right?

For example, woman... we keeping it real, right? Woman 2 Woman? If you were a queen or of a royal family... Let's use a real-life scenario. Imagine that YOU are Duchess Meghan who wed Prince Harry this past summer...

- Would you sell your body for monetary gain? No, cause your kingdom has access to flowing currency.
- Would you belittle and disrespect yourself,

pleasuring yourself with men as you choose and not waiting on a spouse who would become king and promote the kingdom that your Father established?

- Would degrade the other women in your kingdom because they do not possess what you possess, or would you provide opportunity for them to succeed? If you were a queen, there would be no competition...no THOUGHT of any such nonsense.

Oh, but you are a queen. Queen Elizabeth in all her splendor (no offense) cannot compare to what you have inherited. When we present ourselves as a living sacrifice to Jesus, we become a part of the royal family and we inherit the blessings of royalty. We become heirs and joint-heirs to His kingdom.

Romans 8:16-17 (NKJV):
The Spirit Himself bears witness with our spirit that we are children of God, and if children, then heirs—heirs of God and joint heirs with Christ, if indeed we suffer with Him, that we may also be glorified together.

Therefore, we must learn and know the code of conduct of the Kingdom. We learn through the words our Father has spoken in the Bible. Our connection to our home comes through learning about the Kingdom. The Bible is our roadmap so that our Father's will can be duplicated in Earth, as it is in Heaven. We must learn what the expectations are of us as being royalty. Our identity is not in how the world sees us but how God sees us. We are royalty though Jesus Christ.

1 Peter 2:9-12 (NLT)

"But you are not like that, for you are a chosen people. You are royal priests, a holy nation, God's very own possession. As a result, you can show others the goodness of God, for he called you out of the darkness into his wonderful light. "Once you had no identity as a people; now you are God's people. Once you received no mercy; now you have received God's mercy." Dear friends, I warn you as "temporary residents and foreigners" to keep away from worldly desires that wage war against your very souls. Be careful to live properly among your unbelieving neighbors. Then even if they accuse you of doing wrong, they will see your honorable behavior, and they will give honor to God when he judges the world."

Take your rightful place and be who your Father has called you to be.

You were chosen for this. You were created to be in this position before you were even placed in your mother's womb. Your family ties are strong. Your lineage possesses power beyond measure. There is no one or nothing that can come against it...unless YOU allow it! Do not throw the stem away. Remain connected. Without your connection, you cannot do anything.

SCRIPTURE

John 15:1-5 (NIV)
"I am the true vine, and my Father is the gardener. He cuts off every branch in me that bears no fruit, while every branch that does bear fruit, he prunes so that it will be even more fruitful. You are already clean because of the word I have spoken to you. Remain in me, as I also remain in you. No branch can bear fruit by itself; it must remain in the vine. Neither can you bear fruit unless you remain in me. "I am the vine; you are the branches. If you remain in me and I in you, you will bear much fruit; apart from me you can do nothing."

AFFIRMATION

- I will remain connected to my home country, where I have citizenship.
- I will diligently learn the expectations as a citizen of the Kingdom of Heaven.
- I will not just read; I will study the laws of my Heavenly home.
- My Father has great expectations of me.
- HE CHOSE ME!
- I. WILL. NOT. LET. HIM. DOWN.

SELF EXAMINATION

When I decided to confess, repent, and change my way of living, I did not know what to do. As a child, I went to church, but not to establish a relationship with Jesus. What did that mean? What did I have to do? Church to me was listening,

praying, waiting for the big "tune-up," and then seeing everyone flying around the building crying, shouting and praising the Lord. At the age of 22, I felt there was more to this than what I had experienced. Since I had developed study habits from attending college, I decided to approach this new relationship like a course. I was going to STUDY this man named Jesus. Listen, if you were like me, when you made that first step, you were so excited that you wanted to read the entire Bible front to back. However, I soon learned that there were some words I just could not pronounce and did not know what they meant – even with a college degree and in school for a second one. I was like: "Who is 'thee, thou, thine, henceforth, ye, Selah'?" Then the Pastor suggested to stay in the New Testament. Learn about who you say you represent. Learn about Jesus's entire life (Matthew – John). You can also read Psalms for encouragement. Proverbs read like a riddle, so I stayed away from that book until I matured as well. I say that to encourage you. You must know who you are, whose you are, and WHO HE IS! Faith comes by hearing the word of God, but after you hear it, you need to do it and you need to know it. Such that when you are not within the walls of the sanctuary, you can hear the Spirit speak to you through the word of God, because that is how He speaks. When you recognize this, reading the Bible will not feel like a chore, but rather an opportunity to hear your Father and share an intimate moment with Him; like an anxious child waiting for the breaking of day, to unwrap presents on Christmas Day. I shared this information in hopes of helping you in this section of self-examination.

1. How often do you read?

2. How do you choose what to read?
3. What is your purpose for reading the Bible?
    a. Set aside time to meet with your Father, until it becomes routine (before bed – not in bed, before work, on lunch break, etc.).

Note: I am my Father's keeper.

Reflections

Reflections

_____
_____
_____
_____
_____
_____
_____
_____
_____
_____
_____
_____
_____
_____
_____
_____
_____
_____
_____
_____
_____
_____

Reflections

Reflections

Reflections

_____
_____
_____
_____
_____
_____
_____
_____
_____
_____
_____
_____
_____
_____
_____
_____
_____
_____
_____
_____

PART THREE
the Pulp

— the Pulp —

GOAL:
TELL YOUR FLESH TO SHUT UP!

THE Pulp OF THE APPLE

The pulp of the apple is also known as the flesh. It is just underneath the skin. It is the sweetest of the apple and contains the largest amount of the nutrients.

THE Flesh OF THE HUMAN

Our flesh is just underneath the skin as well. The human flesh consists of muscle, tissue and fat (I seem to have more of the latter than the muscle, due to this child-bearing process... humph). Biblically speaking, the reference of the flesh relates to following after desires that are not in alignment with God's principles.

WOMAN 2 WOMAN

Listennn!!! This flesh thing just gets us all in trouble. I wrote a book entitled: "Shut up and Sit Down: A Candid Conversation with the Flesh." You must be open and honest with yourself. If you will not be honest with you, how can you be transparent and humble with God? It is not solely about sexual desires. Are you being a good steward over what God has given you?

Your job, your children, your spouse, your money? Do you make wise decisions or act on impulse and emotion and then whine when your needs are not met?

It has been made VERY clear that if we do what we want to do, we have no parts with the Lord:

Romans 8:8 (NKJV)
So then, those who are in the flesh cannot please God.

The word of God gives specific details on what being in the flesh resembles, in Galatians the fifth chapter. Let's return to the temple discussion that we had when we discussed The Skin. God regards our bodies as sacred, but how do we regard our own bodies?

Woman! We are keeping it real, right? That is why this is called Woman 2 Woman!

You cannot get involved with a man who is an outlaw to the Kingdom. Everything your Father has established for his Kingdom, of which you have access to, THIS man goes contrary. He even talks about your Father and your brother Jesus to your face – and you appear to be comfortable with this? Girl, you cannot be comfortable in this, or you forfeit your rite to the Kingdom promises. You are a queen. If he cannot respect the crown that you wear from the Kingdom that you represent, this dude cannot have access to the jewels (where are the emoji eyes please and thank you)! And, he cannot have access to the jewels without proof of citizenship, permission from the King, and the appropriate ceremony. Us queens have standards given to us by our Father and He is

unwilling to make exceptions simply because His baby girl really, really likes this guy. Your Father loves you so much that He had someone DIE for you. No way, will He lose you to a man – BOOM!

How we behave, speak, and what we allow into this sacred shrine through our eyes and ears are also critically important so that we do NOT defile the temple. The things we say, the things we do, how we converse with one another, the lack of respect we show one another as children of God – what would we expect to experience in a temple? The Holy Spirit hears and sees through you. Perhaps this example will make things a bit clearer.

The White House is where the President of the United States resides during his term. It consists of Secret Service Agents. You are only allowed to enter with an invite. This house is guarded day and night. Within the White House, there is an inner chamber for the President himself. While there may be many rooms, there is only one main room for him to meet with his close cabinet. Tourists plan vacations, schools plan trips, people from around the world come to visit this national monument where the President and his family resides. It stands for a symbol of democracy and freedom, so they say. In detail, the White House is comprised of: 132 rooms, 32 bathrooms, 6 levels, 412 doors, 147 windows, 28 fireplaces, 7 stair cases and 3 elevators and 1 inner room – main chamber, called the Oval office- the office of The President.

Just as the White House is guarded by the Secret Service Agents, our bodies are guarded by the spiritual secret service (his angels). It is also regarded as a temple- a sacred place of

worship for the President of our soul. When there is a breach in security (sin), the alarm sounds and a warning is sent. Just as there are secret passages and doorways for the President and his family to escape, in case of an attack, The Holy Spirit provides a way for us to escape a spiritual attack of sin (I Corinthians 10:13), to prevent the enemy from entering our sacred temple. The Holy Spirit wants to be where you are, but our own will and fleshly desires have separated us from Him.

God wants to be where we are. Do you want Him there?

John 14:23 (NIV)
Jesus replied, "Anyone who loves me will obey my teaching. My Father will love them, and we will come to them and make our home with them.

SCRIPTURE:

---

1 Peter 2:11 (NLT)
Dear friends, I warn you as "temporary residents and foreigners" to keep away from worldly desires that wage war against your very souls.

AFFIRMATION

- I will control myself.
- I will not subject myself to mediocre thoughts and conversations.
- I deserve to be happy and to be loved.
- I love myself and will treat myself with kindness by not allowing others to mistreat me.

SELF-EXAMINATION

You can control yourself. An author by the name of Dan Sullivan talks about the 4C's Formula. It pertains to business and marketing, but I think it is applicable to our discussion as well, so I'm gone put my little spin on it. The 4 C's are: Commit, Courage, Capability, and Confidence.

COMMIT:

Commit to who you want to be. If you desire to a reliable friend, a woman of integrity, a woman of wisdom, well-versed in the word, and peaceful; commit to what it takes to becoming that person. Commit to not giving in to anything that goes against the word, and nobody has to tell you what those things are. You already know. You know you get that feeling. Girl stop ignoring that feeling and just do not do it. Grow out of that.

COURAGE:

Is your willingness to step outside of who you already think you are. In other words, stretching yourself beyond yourself. To change who you are, you must be all in. Dispel the negative thoughts of, "What if this does not work?" and replace it with, "What if it does work?" Have you fully committed to living for Jesus? If you truly have, He will give you the courage to walk away from temptation and He will help you.

CAPABILITY:

You have the ability to be who God desires for you to be. We make it hard, but it is as simple as this: If you did not have the ability, why would you be here? Growing your capability sets up new learning abilities. Learn what you are capable of in

Jesus and own it. Be that and be good at that. When you use the gifts that you already have, new habits and new courage will emerge.

CONFIDENCE:

Confidence is a by-product of capability. Once you realize that you are capable and that you can do all things through Christ, you make bigger commitments, you become stronger in your faith, you become stronger in the word, you witness bigger breakthroughs from challenges in your life that you never thought you could overcome, and you are unwilling to compromise the weight of glory (anointing) that your Father, through Jesus Christ, has graced you with.

1. Do I really want help?
2. What steps do I need to take (disconnect from, connect with)?
3. During moments of temptation, what are some things that I can do?

Reflections

Reflections

Reflections

Reflections

Reflections

Reflections

Reflections

_____
_____
_____
_____
_____
_____
_____
_____
_____
_____
_____
_____
_____
_____
_____
_____
_____
_____
_____

PART FOUR
the Seed

—the Seed—

GOAL:
USE YOUR SEEDS TO PRODUCE FLOWERS, NOT WEEDS

THE *Seed* OF THE APPLE

The seed of the apple is found in the core and can be planted and used to produce more fruit but if consumed in its current state, it produces a deadly poison called cyanide. When large amounts of cyanide are digested it can kill you. Therefore, the seed must be handled properly.

THE *Seed* OF THE HUMAN

The core of who you are determines what you do. At the core of an apple is the seed. At the core of a woman are the seeds that were planted throughout her life.

WOMAN 2 WOMAN

What is the strength of a woman? The strength of a woman is the core of who she is!

The strength of a woman is her foundation and where everything comes from — her core. The core is established by God. God said before we were formed in the womb, he knew who we were. That means our purpose was already

determined. Since the core is already there, it is the value that you will bring to the core of who God made you to be, that defines who you will become, which is called the CORE VALUES.

Woman! This means that you must have a source for your values! If you reflect upon your life and the many things you had to overcome, you will be able to remember the values that someone added to the core of who you are.

Core Values are fundamental (basic) beliefs that define you. No one can take them. You always revert back to your core values regardless of what is happening around you. They keep you stable and grounded.

Every movement of the physical body comes from the core; every strong move, every balance move, rising from a seated position, every movement. Sitting from a standing position, your core muscles must be stable and strengthened enough to support your movement. Spiritually speaking, everything you have experienced, every battle you have won, every giant you have defeated, every victory you have claimed, came from the strength of your core. The core is where you draw strength from and your strength comes from the word of God. Remember who you are — never allow a situation to cause you to compromise who you are. The core of who you are should bring you back to what you were/are founded upon. Maybe you did not have a mother in your life or a dad in your life; but you had someone. You had a grandmother, you had a teacher, you had a sibling, you had a friend who had a mother, you had an uncle, you had someone. God placed someone in your life, at some point IN your life, to add value to your core.

What is on the inside of you can either kill you or grow you, based on how your core is nurtured; therefore, your core must be handled with care.

I had an epiphany moment in my life, which ultimately led to the Woman 2 Woman Conference, journal, and soon to be available the book. This is journal is entitled a "journey" journal with intent. Not only do I hope to somehow help you on your journey, but in the process, I am strengthening myself, understanding who I am, and working on my areas of weaknesses.

The summer of 2018, I was headed home from the grocery store and received some news. My husband is a Pastor and has been overseeing a congregation that his grandparents founded in 1973. I had learned that someone was leaving the ministry and going to be a part of another ministry. It was not for any ill reason, simply because they felt they were being led to join another church. Although there were no issues, no drama, nothing, I felt hurt. I wondered why. I started evaluating areas of the ministry and if we could have done anything different that would prevent this person from feeling they needed to go elsewhere. Suddenly, my mind began to drift back to when my mom and dad separated. Her words rang in my head. As I stood at the door with my mom, my dad facing us from the outside (me being 4 years old was what I was told) my mom told my dad to get his shoes and leave. She said that I echoed what she said: "Get your shoes daddy." From that point on, I was detached from my dad without a reason; disconnected.

Throughout my life, as I have explained in previous books,

my mother never said anything bad about my dad. As I became of age, I tried reaching out to have a relationship. What seemed to be a fresh start, resulted in a dead end. At that moment, I realized what was connected to my core. The values instilled in me were about being independent, being educated, and being saved. Those are what I like to call spiritual and professional values. The moral value that was attached to my core, as a result of this, affected every aspect of my life as it relates to relationships. Moral values are a set of principles that guide a person in identifying what is right or wrong. Some moral values are identified as having integrity, compassion, courage, honesty, perseverance, respectfulness and responsibility. In just 15 minutes of driving, I had an epiphany, an "ah-ha" moment. I had detachment issues.

Throughout my life, when dealing with issues in relationships, I always wondered what I did wrong or why did I have to get treated unfairly. I was always carrying the blame even when I was not at fault. I was always wondering why, what did I do wrong, what could I have done differently. This mindset prevented me from being me. It kept me on pins and needles with people and relationships. This detachment mess ultimately affected my self-esteem, my willingness to connect with people or allow them to get close to me.

On the other hand, it made me want to do whatever I could to see others happy. Whatever was in my possession to do, I would do and still do. Throughout school I became a people-pleaser just to fit in, and I became more introverted – because I never understood the why behind the why at 4 years old. Attached to my core was and is a stinky detachment issue

that affects the way I engage with people. Now that I realize it, I know how to manage both it and me. I understand that while I may mistakes, because I am not perfect, I did not make ALL of the mistakes.

My mom unexpectedly passed away June 12, 2017. It was and is one of the hardest things I have had to endure. Even harder than losing a child. She never told me why she and dad separated. My dad is still around. We both live in the same city and I don't imagine ever getting a "why" from him. What matters is I thank God that He is a loving Father and cared enough for me to show me my weaknesses and what is connected to my core that prevents me from being who He has predestined for me to be. I encourage you to do the same. Abandonment, molestation, loneliness, loss of a loved one, guilt, shame, depression, stress, anxiety, disease, guilt by association, weight gain, weight loss, failed relationships, decisions based on emotions and fear, these are all attacks from the kingdom of darkness attempting to weaken your core. We often hear others say not to look back. This time sis, it is okay to look back, if its purpose is to push you forward.

SCRIPTURE

Psalm 27:10 (NLT)
Even if my father and mother abandon me, the Lord will hold me close.

AFFIRMATION

- I am free to create the life that I desire.
- I speak my truth with confidence and courage.

- I take full responsibility of my wellness.
- I am well in my mind, body, and spirit.

SELF-EXAMINATION

Take a journey back in time. Jot down all the hurtful things that you experienced in your life.

Circle only one that affected you the most. This is an important step into knowing who you are and why you move the way that you do.

1. What happened?
2. How did you feel?
3. How do you feel now, years, months, weeks later?
4. Were you abandoned? Taken advantage of? Isolated? How has that incident shaped your life?
5. What are you willing to do to regain control over this portion of your life?

Note: What you need to be the best you is already on the inside of you. You will have to be intentional to tap into it.

Reflections

Reflections

Reflections

Reflections

Reflections

Reflections

Reflections

— Summary —

— Summary —

HOW DO YOU STRENGTHEN YOUR CORE?

If you have been in church circles long enough, then I know you have read this particular chapter before. It's likely been used as the measuring stick of womanhood. Sometimes, even to shame and disgrace the women who don't measure up to these standards. Of course, it is the Proverbs 31 woman. I want to focus on ONE particular verse in this chapter that sets the tone for the entire chapter.

Proverbs 31:17 (NKJV)
She girds herself with strength and strengthens her arms.

We never learn of this woman's background and her upbringing and I believe there is a reason for this. The reason is that IT REALLY DOESN'T MATTER. God can take the mess you came from and make you virtuous for HIS glory. Just like the prodigal son came to his senses, this woman did as well. The virtuous woman had to talk to herself and tell herself what was gone be, somewhere in her life's journey. In order to gird herself, she had to get her mind right. At some point, she heard about a man named Jesus. She recalled to her mind and she put the action behind what she was thinking.

Have you ever seen a girdle? I have 5 children. Everybody don't have a "snatchback" body, as they say. My body did not snatch itself back together after the 3rd child (somebody

please bring the emoji eyes here and now). When I need everything to hold itself in place and I need help sucking and tucking in my gut, I wear my girdle and I have them in all shapes and sizes – in Jesus name (emoji eyes please).

A girdle binds my stomach together. In fact, the word girdle is derived from the word GIRD.

The Proverbs 31 woman girded her loins. Gird means to secure, surround, equip or get into position (new emoji alert: the dancing lady). Loins are physically considered the upper and lower abdominal area.

Why would she gird her loins with strength? Why would the Proverbs 31, virtuous woman, need to support her loins and make them strong?

Because everything she had to do from verse 10-31 required strength from her core, which is the strength of a woman:

> The strength of a woman is her core (aka the loins).
>
> Her core is her foundation.
>
> Her foundation is the word of God.
>
> The word of God is the truth.
>
> The truth is of the utmost importance in the life of a Christian because Jesus is the truth. Jesus says I am the way, the truth, and the life – no man comes to the Father but by me (John 14:6).

Woman you are in a battle. The enemy is trying to attack the core of who you are and where you draw strength from. If you disconnect from the Kingdom, you have no army fighting for you; you fight alone. But when you strengthen (gird) your

core (loins) with the truth (word), your foundation cannot be shaken.

It is so easy to look at the condition of our world, our country, our state, city, communities and even within our own families and feel hopeless due to all of the adversity we are surrounded by. The appearance of evil is more prevalent than good. No one chooses to fully commit to the statutes of God. Nobody desires to truly forgive and let go. There are all sorts of division in the body of religion (not Christ). After all this chaos and thoughts of hopelessness, you'll soon begin to wonder if God even cares. If not careful, we will carry the mindset of quitting and giving up.

I just wanted to encourage you to strengthen your core, woman. That is where your strength lies.

We all mourn; we all go through, but we can get through only when we strengthen our core. Make Jesus your foundation. What are you going to do to get up again?

As believers there is a cross we must bear. All that means is that there is something that we will have to go through and learn how to get through, but we can't get through alone. We scratch, claw, grasp and pull, to stand. The Bible says having done ALL to stand...STAND! My posture may be a bit slouched. My shoulders may be rounded instead of up and back, but when I have on the belt of truth, my core is stable. The Bible says; Having done all to stand, stand. You gone have to make up in your mind and tell yourself: "I don't know what tomorrow will bring. I do not know what the next year has in store, but I do know this: The word is nigh thee (it is right

here). It is the word of faith that is being discussed right now. If I confess with my mouth the Lord Jesus and I believe in my heart that my Father raised Jesus from the dead, I will be saved. I have a Father who is uncompromising, relentless and unwilling to give up on me."

The virtuous woman girds her loins with strength. Well isn't that something. Ephesians 6:14 says: Stand therefore, having your loins girt about with truth, and having on the breastplate of righteousness. My loins are my core. The strength of a woman resides in the value that she adds to her core and it must be founded upon the principles of God.

Skin of the physical body serves as protection. Our skin protects our pulp – also known as the flesh. Underneath the skin is your flesh, organs, sinews, bone marrow and blood. Bones (stem) holds the body together. But the seed – the core of who you are is your soul.

Woman, strengthen your core.

Ephesians 6:13-18 The Message (MSG)
Be prepared. You're up against far more than you can handle on your own. Take all the help you can get, every weapon God has issued, so that when it's all over but the shouting you'll still be on your feet. Truth, righteousness, peace, faith, and salvation are more than words. Learn how to apply them. You'll need them throughout your life. God's Word is an indispensable weapon. In the same way, prayer is essential in this ongoing warfare. Pray hard and long. Pray for your brothers and sisters. Keep your eyes open. Keep each other's spirits up so that no one falls behind or drops out.

Reflections

Reflections

Reflections

_____
_____
_____
_____
_____
_____
_____
_____
_____
_____
_____
_____
_____
_____
_____
_____
_____
_____

Reflections

_____
_____
_____
_____
_____
_____
_____
_____
_____
_____
_____
_____
_____
_____
_____
_____
_____
_____
_____
_____

Reflections

_____
_____
_____
_____
_____
_____
_____
_____
_____
_____
_____
_____
_____
_____
_____
_____
_____
_____

Reflections

Reflections

References

Unless otherwise indicated, all Scripture quotations are from the King James Version (KJV)

Bible, King James Version (NKJV)

Bible, New Living Translation (NLT)

Bible, New International Version (NIV)

Bible, King James Version (MSG)

Bible, King James Version (CEB)

Bible, King James Version (AMP)

(1) Ince DeWitt, Sarah (2018). Parts of a fruit: The apple. Retrieved from https://www.hunker.com/13428118/parts-of-a-fruit-the-apple

(2) "Gird." Meriam-Webster.com. 2018.
https://www.merriam-webster.com (15 Nov 2018)

(3) "Loin." Meriam-Webster.com. 2018.
https://www.merriam-webster.com (15 Nov 2018

(4) "Flesh." Meriam-Webster.com. 2018.
https://www.merriam-webster.com (15 Nov 2018)

(5) "Skin." Meriam-Webster.com. 2018.
https://www.merriam-webster.com (15 Nov 2018)

(6) "Flesh." Meriam-Webster.com. 2018.
https://www.merriam-webster.com (15 Nov 2018)

(7) Sullivan, Dan. The 4 C's Formula: Commitment Courage Capability and Confidence.

www.ingramcontent.com/pod-product-compliance
Lightning Source LLC
Chambersburg PA
CBHW040624300426
43661CB00146B/1001